Casa Dos Cisnes

A Colonial Mexican Home Reimagined For Modern Living

Puerto Vallarta, Mexico

Casa Dos Cisnes

PuertoVallartaLuxuryVilla.com

TWO SWANS MEDIA
PuertoVallartaLuxuryVilla.com

2443 Fillmore Street #9115-380
San Francisco, California 94115

© 2018 Casa Dos Cisnes
All rights reserved.

ISBN: 978-0-9600263-0-2

No part of this publication may be reproduced, distributed, or transmitted in any form or by any means, including photocopying, recording, or other electronic or mechanical methods, without the prior written permission of the publisher, except in the case of brief quotations embodied in reviews and certain other non-commercial uses permitted by copyright law.

Contents

Preface 5
The Story

Chapter 1 13
**Architectural Features -
The Vision Becomes Reality**

Chapter 2 47
Other Highlights of Casa Dos Cisnes

Chapter 3 59
Casa Dos Cisnes - A Way of Living

Preface - The Story

Every space tells a story. Carved into a mountainside, a ten-minute drive south of Puerto Vallarta, Casa Dos Cisnes is a dazzling expression of the artistic vision and elegant lifestyle of its owners. As much a mindset as a physical construct, the "House of Two Swans" is a colonial-style compound designed for tranquil indoor-outdoor living. Casa Dos Cisnes transcends the notion of architecture as a mere enclosure from the world and redefines the personal domicile as an emotional structure that is intimately connected to the land.

For the owners and their guests, Casa Dos Cisnes embodies the quintessential tropical fantasia. Unfurling over four stories, exquisite living spaces marry traditional colonial features with modern decorative details to form a holistic integration of architecture, interiors and terrain in a family retreat that provides comfortable year-round living. Boasting state-of-the-art amenities, the villa provides unbridled comfort and convenience without intruding on the natural beauty that surrounds it.

With deserted beaches overseen by jungle covered mountains, Mexico's Pacific Coast possesses a flamboyant natural beauty that has long provided architects and designers with inspiration and an outlet for their creative energies. Infused with light and invigorated by ocean breezes, Casa Dos Cisnes takes its design cues from the rugged topography of the Sierra Madre and Mexico's magical color palette. Throughout the magnificent residence, every space is immersed in the azure colors of the ocean, the earthy tones of the desert, the amber glow of the setting sun, the infinite green shades of tropical forest and the kaleidoscopic hues of the market place.

Façade

With its blank public face—a flat stucco wall painted in shades of white and burnt orange—surmounted with a cupola and crucifix, Casa Dos Cisnes' façade belies the theatrical scale and decorative riches within.

Best appreciated through the senses, Casa Dos Cisnes evokes a spiritual style of architecture that invites one to embrace every life-affirming moment. In the main living spaces, walls, doors and sharp angles are shunned in favor of sensual curves and archways that provide unobstructed Pacific Ocean vistas. The dining room awakens the appetite for gourmet Mexican cuisine created by the villa's in-house chef, the master bedroom invites rest and serenity, the sitting room inspires intimate conversation. Whether it's breakfast on the patio surrounded by tropical birds, sun salutations on the terrace or a refreshing dip in the infinity pool, Casa Dos Cisnes is a pleasure seeker's paradise.

The owner's design pays homage to Mexico's rich history, tradition and mysticism. From lavish bathrooms adored with custom glazed *talavera* tiles to stately tables set with exquisite ceramics, fat-bellied pots from Tlaquepaque, *cantera* stone columns, furniture *hecho a mano,* weeping walls, and a profusion of tropical plants, Casa dos Cisnes presents a brilliant synthesis of Mexico's many cultural influences. But for all its aesthetic perfection and historic elements, the villa rejects the cold façade of a museum. Rather the home projects the warmth of the owners' spiritual, physical and emotional lives. Casa Dos Cisnes offers an original way of living, a soulful haven where family, friends and guests can indulge in the eternal fantasy of sophisticated ocean living, for a few days at least.

Doorway

A venerable doorway leads to an enclosed courtyard that forms a vivid microcosm of Mexican life. Exterior doors are constructed from the most durable hardwoods, including mesquite and sabino, which are praised for their density and natural resistance to insect infestation.

Courtyard

Upon entering the courtyard with its Mudejar-style fountains, tropical plants and flowers, one immediately feels the mystique and harmony that defines the Spanish colonial-style courtyard. Providing architectural balance and functionality, the courtyard allows light and tropical breezes to emanate through a mosaic of intimate spaces and communal living areas.

Cisnes living/ dining view

Appointed with comfortable furnishings, the villa's living spaces merge imperceptibly with Mexico's fabled Pacific coastline and provide a showcase for the owner's personal collection of artwork, sculptures and antiquities.

Traditional clay pots by staircase

A showcase for crafts from every state in Mexico, Casa Dos Cisnes triumphs the time-honored skills and boundless imagination of Mexico's master craftsmen.

Terraza comedor / Dining terrace

An elaborate archway of cantera stone frames the transcendent views of Banderas Bay. Comfortable wicker furniture and tropical foliage provides an earthly contrast to the home's arresting religious iconography. At Casa Dos Cisnes, daily rituals are transformed into heavenly experiences.

Courtyard fountain

The home's innumerable water features speak to the Moor's influence upon Spanish colonial style homes from the 8th century.

Puerto Vallarta

With its balmy climate, exotic flora and fauna, isolated beaches, jungled clothed mountains, and rich culinary heritage, the quaint village of Puerto Vallarta has cast an instantaneous spell since the 1960s.

CASA DOS CISNES

Chapter 1
Architectural Features - The Vision Becomes Reality

We have our own architecture, we don't need refried châteaux.

José Clemente Orozco

Part 1
Colonial Style

Mexico's complicated architectural legacy stems from a rich cultural tapestry that fused the indigenous culture of the Aztec, Maya and Toltecs with Baroque Spanish and French colonial style. The colonial era of Mexico, or New Spain, spanned three centuries (1521-1821) and bore witness to a multitude of styles and innovations in European architecture. The fantastical imagination of Mexico's indigenous population layered upon the Baroque flourishes of traditional Spanish forms gave birth to a colorful style that has become an iconic, and very fashionable, design ethos. Mexico's rich and varied landscape—mystical jungles, majestic mountain ranges, austere deserts, high plains, spluttering volcanoes and gaping canyons—finds expression in peaked roof lines, undulating walls, vaulted ceilings and a vivid color palette that echoes the glow of the rising sun, the iridescence of the ocean and the lushness of the jungle.

Terraza comedor / Dining terrace

The covered patio area, or terraza comedor, embellished with a series of nichos that showcase religious artifacts, provides a divine setting for a traditional Mexican breakfast. An archway supported by cantera columns provides unobstructed views of the Conchas Chinas neighborhood and the dramatic coastline of Banderas Bay.

In Mexico, the colonial home represented the Moor's urge to defend his home and family from threats of the human and natural kind. With a plain facade framed by inscrutable high walls, windows laced with ironwork and a colossal wooden door worthy of the Alhambra Palace, the prototypical Mexican colonial home turned in on itself and deterred scrutiny. The home's antechamber, or *zaguán*, led to the courtyard—the beating heart of the home—where plants and water features were surrounded by arches (*portales*) and hallways (*corredores*). Landscape design with integrated irrigation technology evolved from Muslim traditions and spiritual practices in ancient Persia. Islamic garden design is employed by an axial plan with a central water feature. Based on the idea of the chahārbāgh (literally "four gardens"), four-quadrant courtyard gardens emulate the four rivers of paradise from the Koran. In the 8th century, when Islam spread into southern Spain, Islamic Spain (also known as Al-Andalus or modern Andalusia) became a showcase for the evolution of a sophisticated use of water for both practical and aesthetic uses.

These Spanish gardening traditions were then exported to the colonies, including Mexico.

Typically, the ground floor, which featured the living room, dining room and kitchen, comprised the theater of the home from which all collective activity would pivot. A stone stairway led to an upper enclave, the owner's private living quarters adorned with decorative elements that bore all the hallmarks of a hierarchical society that associated European style with wealth and power. The service areas of the home were relegated to the lower floors of the villa. The Mexican Revolution of 1910-1920 ushered in a new spirit of nationalism. The post-revolutionary government of Alvaro Obregón cultivated a sense of national identity for the new republic. Artists such as Rivera, Rufino Tamayo, and Chucho Reyes established collections of Hispanic art and decorated their homes in the "popular" Indian style. Because of their influence, interior decorators began to substitute Mexican colonial and indigenous furniture and art for luxuries from Paris.

Dining Room/ Mirror

The intelligent placement of a mirror in the dining room ensures that everyone at the table can revel in the moonlit views of the bay.

Master bedroom: Day view

The home's crowning achievement, the master bedroom is a stunning synthesis of traditional Mexican design, religious iconography and modern comforts, all suspended in a dreamlike setting that feels immune to the passing of time.

There is an Indian proverb that says that everyone is a house with four rooms, a physical, a mental, an emotional, and a spiritual. Most of us tend to live in one room most of the time but unless we go into every room every day, even if only to keep it aired, we are not a complete person.
Rumer Godden

Part 2
A Colonial Home Reimagined for Modern Living

At Casa Dos Cisnes, Mexico's rich architectural legacy is reimagined for the 21st century. Behind a venerable hand-carved wooden door, *cantera* columns stand like sentinels around the perimeter of a beautiful courtyard from which light is metered out in doses, color brightening and intensifying the atmosphere of the living spaces that surround it. Woven through the courtyard's four levels, potted plants and flowers invite communion with nature, *talavera* encrusted fountains and weeping walls recall the Moorish influence upon Spain, and the voluptuous curves of hand-made claypots speak to Mexico's rich artisan tradition.

Casa Dos Cisnes offers a unique interpretation of vernacular architecture. While the Spanish colonial home in Mexico was typically designed according to a "U" - or "L"-shaped template, Casa Dos Cisnes' three-sided courtyard establishes

Painting

In the hallway, a reproduction of the Virgen del Apocalipsis *by Juan Correa (1646-1716) hangs above an antique colonial period table fashioned from an oxen yolk, found in the state of Jalisco.*

light as the home's primal force. Positioned between the street and principal living spaces, the courtyard is where all worlds overlap and entwine–owners, staff, guests, visitors–and from where the architectural features of the living spaces expand seamlessly into the landscape, united by the astonishing panoramas of the Pacific Ocean.

Good design creates a progression between privacy and transparency. The high-ceilinged spaces of the main living room and formal dining room and the covered patio area, or *terraza comedor*, are unhindered by walls or sharp angles. The owner's goal was to fashion an exquisite home that was sophisticated enough for formal entertaining but adaptable enough to lend itself to a relaxed, family-friendly arrangement. While the stately living and dining room are expansive enough to host weddings, special events and family dinner parties, the villa's alcoves, retreat rooms and versatile furnishings (the dining table can be expanded to seat from four to 12) invite romance and personal contemplation.

Adjacent to the living room, an informal sitting room forms an interface or neutral territory between the home's private and public realms. In addition to showcasing the owners' stunning collection of clay pots from Tonalá and Tlaquepaque and book collection, the sitting room provides a relaxed backdrop for intimate conversation. The master suite above the entrance floor and the four bedrooms spread across the lower third and fourth floors provide appropriately proportioned sleeping quarters; not so big as to overcome the gravitational pull of the living area, not too small as to preclude comfort and relaxation.

The quintessential 21st-century American home often focuses on scale and grandeur. At Casa Dos Cisnes, a balance and grace to the décor and a harmony between architectural form and function underscores the home's architectural precepts. For the design of Casa Dos Cisnes, the owners turned their attention to the quality of each decorative detail and architectural element to create a villa that is big on soul rather than an exercise in excess. Artfully juxtaposed against comfortable rancho-style furnishings, colonial reproduction paintings lend an aristocratic allure. The clever positioning of mirrors and candles and a symmetrical constellation of art, crafts and mementoes, ensures that a balance between the home's positive and negative spaces prevails. During the day, ocean views provide the living-dining room's dramatic focal point. By night, the interplay of moonlight, the elemental warmth of the monumental fireplace, candles and the masterful use of indirect, recessed light sets the stage for cocktails, conversation and exquisite, nouveau Mexican cuisine.

Away room

Adjacent to the master bedroom, natural and traditional materials impart warmth to the cozy retreat room off of the master bedroom, a quiet, informal space to read, work or simply listen to your own pulse

Master retreat balcony

Visible from the courtyard, on the home's upper level, the master retreat room features a Juliet balcony. A traditional, low hanging red-tiled roof and traditional beams reveal the colonial influence upon the design of Casa Dos Cisnes.

Living area view with fireplace

In the living room, a cantera *stone fireplace provides the room's focal point while decorative statement pieces shimmer day and night.*

Dining Room Chandelier

A chandelier completes the dining room like a piece of jewelry and forms the centerpiece for epic dining.

Pool terrace entertainment

Multiple outdoor entertaining spaces expand the communal areas of the home that are traditionally centered upon a formal dining room or, more specifically, the dining room table.

Dining room/ living room

The use of solid walls is kept to a minimum throughout the communal living area providing open, yet comfortable spaces in which to socialize.

View from *terraza comedor*

The ambient warmth of the tropics causes architectural distinctions between indoors and outside to evaporate, along with the walls that divide them.

Living room at night

A fireplace carved from cantera stone anchors the communal living area and establishes harmony with the architectural elements of the courtyard. Around the fireplace, candles and cove lighting in the bóveda ceiling create a romantic ambience that echoes the warm colors and forms of the architecture.

Part 3
Night and Day

*V*isual beauty emanates from the interplay of light as each day and evening emerges. Thoughtfully designed lighting reveals the elegance of the architecture's forms and rhythms and accentuates the subtle colors and textures of materials. Light embraces and unifies each distinct element that composes the space. At Casa Dos Cisnes, the owners demonstrate a keen awareness of this inextricable relationship between material object and light. Throughout the home, lighting responds to the needs of a space. The transformation of experiential spaces brings to life an environment that lifts the spirit and nurtures the soul by day and by night.

When it comes to lighting, one of Casa Dos Cisnes' most laudable characteristics is that nothing is overdesigned; the quality of light is more important than the choice of light fixture. Non-intrusive lights are nestled into soffits where they softly wash light over a wall or an archway, or they're obscured within columns or cabinets to highlight a stunning *bóveda* ceiling. A focal glow commands attention and distinguishes the important from the unimportant, the negative from the positive space.

The central courtyard at night

Throughout the home, various light sources are layered to create a warm, romantic ambience that spotlights the home's focal points and statement pieces without compromising the radiant energy that prevails in the principal living spaces.

Living area at night

During the day, breathtaking ocean views command full attention in the living room. By night, skilled lighting techniques transform the public spaces into a lavish stage set for lively conversation and cocktails followed by a Mexican culinary odyssey. The ocher walls mutate into a soft pink tone that blends with the tiled floor draped with a hand woven rug from Temoaya.

Accent lighting

In the courtyard, clever accent lighting illuminates colonial crosses and rosaries hanging above a colonial style bench.

Courtyard at night

Light is layered using a combination of lighting sources to create a cohesive and versatile lighting system that fashions a complex space that is both functional and emotionally satisfying. Soft ambient, direct or indirect lighting renders the home's singular/distinctive Mexican features in an infinite arrangement of cinematic permutations: the studs on a hand carved doorway; the crepuscular glow of a *talavera* tile; the shimmer of hand blown goblets; the brushstrokes of a colonial painting; the worn patina of a crucifix.

Light is also effectively employed to distinguish the home's public spaces from its private enclaves while simultaneously unifying multiple spaces into one harmonious entity. Thanks to a thoughtful combination of ambient lighting, candles and recessed lights, solitary and social moments harmoniously coalesce within the same room in an inspiring combination of transparency and opacity.

Courtyard by day

The tension between light and dark, daytime and nighttime, offers a fine example of the owner's adherence to an emotional style of architecture that illustrates their desire to brighten and soften the world.

The living/dining room at twilight

Elemental flickers of light from the colonial hacienda style chandelier and candles positioned throughout the living and dining room create a festive ambience.

Terraza Comedor

Detailed accent lighting is used throughout the home to spotlight artworks, sculptures and Mexican handicrafts. Here in the terraza comedor, nichos illuminated at night by recessed lighting add drama and intensity to the room's arresting religious artifacts.

Bedroom with two queen beds

Recessed lights in the faux-painted ceiling cast a glow over the one bedroom with twin queen-sized beds. The soothing ocher wall color is echoed in vivacious hand-woven serapes that dress the two queen beds and contrast with crisp white linens. The bedroom opens onto the lush interior courtyard where a glorious centerpiece water fountain is a nod to Spain's conquest by the Moors. Over two hand carved bed frames, two crucifixes provides a thematic symmetry that imbues the room with harmony and balance.

View from courtyard over living area

An open three-story courtyard provides daylight and fresh breezes to all rooms. A harmonious open floor plan allows nothing to detract from the ethereal beauty of the home's sun soaked vistas.

Covered patio – accordion-style door feature

A covered patio extends the full length of the home. The owners chose accordion-style doors to maximize light and air flow. The living room and dining area enjoy uninhibited Pacific Coast views regardless of the time of day or season. Discreet accordion-style patio doors provide a wall of light when closed; when open, they fold virtually out of sight.

Twilight view from *terraza comedor*

Recessed lighting in the cantera *stone archway harmoniously blend and subsume the fading light of the sun.*

Colonial period art throughout the villa

Accent lighting illuminates the evocative colonial art displayed throughout Casa Dos Cisnes.

Cove lighting

In the hallway leading to the master bedroom, cove lighting directs light upwards to highlight the exquisite craftsmanship of the vaulted bóveda ceiling.

Part 4
Hillside Location

To live in a villa draped across a cliff top that affords magnificent panoramic views of the ocean is the personification of romantic, luxurious living. A sanctuary that is elevated from the tensions and the crackle and fire of the world below fosters a sense of calm and stirs an affinity for nature. Even before the arrival of the Spanish, cliff top dwellings garnered protection from enemy attack and provided strategic vantage points during times of war and strife. Today, villas that preside over forests, beaches and towns distinguish themselves for their ethereal beauty and privacy. In addition to offering awe-inspiring vistas that excite the body and mind, cliff top houses represent amazing feats of architecture and engineering.

To build a private house on a sheer cliff that has views on every side, requires meticulous design and planning. As Casa Dos Cisnes testifies, the spectacular results are worth it. Reminiscent of a viewing platform for water, land and sky, nature seems to surround every space. The terraced home allows for a compartmentalized living space that establishes a distinct function and mood for each space of the home. Visitors enter from the street on level two (the main floor) which leads to the home's inner

Street and ocean side views of home

To construct a terraced home that takes full advantage of ocean breezes, light and shadow and the seasonal changes of the sun, the entrance to which goes practicably unnoticed from the outside, poses great challenges for architects and designers.

sanctum: the courtyard. The main level is split into three zones defined by the kitchen and an expansive living-dining room, which extends into a covered outdoor patio area that seems to float above the ocean below. A *cantera* staircase leads to the villa's upper level, the homeowner's peaceful sanctuary, complete with a lavish master suite, terrace, and "away" room. From the master bedroom, accordion-style patio doors, with floor-to-ceiling windows allow access to the spacious terrace that invites romance with its outdoor fireplace, intimate dining area and more stunning panoramas. On level three, one floor below the main communal areas, three bedrooms (two with ocean views) and two and a half bathrooms are located along with a media/game room that combines state-of-the-art technology with rustic furnishings. On level four, one finds a fifth bedroom with a private bath. Just below, the home's overtures to modern living find expression in a series of interconnected recreational spaces: a gym; an infinity pool; a wet bar; a covered patio lounge. An outdoor staircase meanders discreetly through the home's gardens to the staff quarters and utility spaces.

Master bedroom terrace

The master terrace provides a private space within the home for sunbathing, an intimate dinner or personal contemplation.

Stunning views from the Master bedroom

On the top level, the villa's master bedroom and terrace, with its heavenly views, is utterly divine.

Striking views from pool patio

Carved from the cliff face, the heated infinity pool is a showcase for the home's superlative terraced design and respect for the site's topography. Surrounded by huge pots of bougainvillea, and framed by forests teeming with flora and fauna, the sound of birdsong or a cocktail shaker, is the frequent acoustical accopaniment to an afternoon of poolside indulgence.

Patio in front of the living room

Terraces and platforms demonstrate structural integrity and provide expansive living spaces that are fully immersed in nature and provide sufficient space for special events, parties and celebrations.

Staircase

Designed as an independent feature of the villa, a dramatic spiral staircase links the four stories of the home. Faux-painted ocher walls adorned with nichos that showcase religious artifacts and personal mementoes, wrap around stairs cut from grey cantera stone.

Part 5
Eclectic marriage of Hacienda and Rancho Style

Designed for a modern lifestyle, it's the small details at Casa Dos Cisnes that transform the stunning structure into a warm and comfortable home that speaks to the owner's nomadic lifestyle, deep knowledge of Mexico's architectural history and passion for Mexican folk art and religious artifacts.

During the 16th century, the formal living style of the Spanish colonialists coalesced with Mexico's untamed landscape and whimsical indigenous forms to create a design ethos known as rancho style. With its comfortable furnishings and balance of strong colors with natural light and air, the owners adopted various tenets of rancho style to temper the strained formality of classical colonial design. Beneath a red tiled roof, deep reddish-brown beams crown exuberant interiors festooned with chandeliers, kaleidoscopic embroidery and an abundance of gold leaf. Innovative artistic accents defy conventional design themes. Hand carved chests and cabinets, which add depth and character to the villa's expansive spaces, hold court with whimsical Day of the Dead sculptures and gilded frescos.

Montage of decorative pieces and artifacts

Throughout Casa Dos Cisnes, Mexican antiquities unite seamlessly with modern design accents.

From whimsical paintings and sculptures, to elaborate friezes, colonial paintings, hand-woven rugs, copper mirrors, talavera tiles, chandeliers, and hand-carved chests, each room delivers its own bravura notes.

Montage of religious artifacts

Filled with relics of celebration and worship, Casa Dos Cisnes pays homage to the pivotal role of religion in Mexican life. A dominant and unifying force, the color and pageantry of fiestas and celebrations relieve the prosaic routines of isolated villages. No home is without multiple crucifixes, statues of saints and religious paintings. Indeed, the saints are considered part of the family and are treated with affection and familiarity.

Courtyard

A modern iteration of the Spanish colonial style and an antidote to McMansion constructs, the residence overflows with its owner's personality. A natural flow between intimate spaces and communal areas adds proportion and balance to the home.

Bathrooms incorporate design elements that resemble water; the blue and turquoise colors, shapes and textures that conjure images of ocean life. Beautiful lustrous hardwoods, hand-wrought iron and copper, stone in kaleidoscopic hues, from pink to grey to green, all blend in inspired combinations with the home's contemporary features.

Throughout Casa Dos Cisnes, there is meaning and symbolism involved in the selection and placement of each object reflecting the Mexican people's innate sense of order and composition. Even in the most humble of villages, symmetry prevails in everything from the thoughtfully arranged fruits and vegetables in the marketplace, to the alignment of structures that flank the main square, or zócalo, to modest homes proudly displaying carefully crafted objects and furniture.

In essence, Casa Dos Cisnes is an ensemble performance of various architectural styles and design philosophies. The owner's rancho style furnishings become an integral part of the villa's colonial structure and design, a spirited mingling of real life relics with modern and custom-made pieces that is simultaneously pure and practical, artful yet unpretentious.

Detail image of chest

Lending warmth to working and living environments, storage elements account for some of the most diverse antiques in Mexico. As in Spain, the chest, which served as a safeguard for valuables and storage for food and clothing, was the single most important item of furniture in early Mexico. The most common woods used for trunks were, and continue to be, Spanish cedar, sabino or Mexican cypress and mesquite.

Detail image of bench

Benches are a popular and symbolic feature of the traditional Mexican home. In courtyards, zócalos and the portals of the plaza, the full view of Mexican life is entirely accessible from a languid shady bench; taking a seat to put the world to rights as the rituals of daily life unfold is a favorite pastime in Mexico.

Retreat Room

Rich hardwoods add depth and character to the rooms. Connecting the master bedroom to the "retreat room," the planks of each wooden door are held together by iron braces and large round-headed clavos, or hand forged nails.

Detail shot of colonial artwork

Colonial work graces the walls of the house reflecting the owner's passion for Mexico colonial art and architecture.

Master bedroom terrace

A fine example of an outdoor space that is private, the master bedroom terrace provides unobstructed views over Banderas Bay. An inviting outdoor fireplace and tables establishes an intimate entertainment space.

Master bedroom

The bedroom is a sanctuary for both its occupants and the religious artifacts it holds. Gilded saints keep vigil ensuring that the bed is the focal point of the room. Walls painted in soft blue tones blend with the ocean below while the bed, dressed in crisp white linens and draped with a hand embroidered serape are balanced with flowing white drapes that reflect the color and contour of ocean waves. Accordion-style doors help to blur the boundaries between inside and outside. Religious artifacts set up a visual contrast between the comfortable furnishings and modern amenities.

Patio by pool

In Mexico, patios typically burst with activity. The work of craftsmen as well as housekeeping is done in an ambience inspired by nature, potted flowers, plants and nature's whimsical additions.

Chapter 2
Other Highlights of Casa Dos Cisnes

Introduction

The style and ingenuity that underscores the architectural elements and design features of the traditional colonial-style home illuminate the Mexican people's harmonious relationship with their environment. For centuries, Mexico's master craftsmen have married beautiful and noble form with function. Even the most mundane, prosaic and functional artifacts are deemed worthy of creative expression. From the multi-hued tones of *cantera* stone to rich and resilient hardwoods, clay, and natural fibre, nature has endowed the nation's artisans with the materials and inspiration to fashion timeless architectural elements as well as an eclectic array of furniture, ceramics, glassworks and religious artifacts. From *nichos* to *cupolas*, fountains to *bóvedas*, *cantera* columns and ambient lighting effects, the traditional Mexican home incorporates a myriad of styles and features that create dramatic visual scale.

Cantera Stone

A predominant feature or embellishment of the Mexican colonial-style home, *cantera* stone (named for the Spanish word for quarry) is a volcanic stone found throughout North America. *Cantera* stone is mined exclusively in various regions of Mexico including Queretaro, Jalisco, Saltillo and Michoacán. According to its origin, it is available in shades of peach, pink, gold, grey and brown. Durable and highly malleable, *cantera* absorbs air and moisture (it is perfect for outdoor spaces) and allows for intricate carving. At Casa Dos Cisnes, *cantera* stone, employed for doorways, fireplaces, fountains, columns and flooring, beguiles with its rugged beauty and soulful antiquity.

Bóveda

A stunning feature of colonial-style homes, the barrel vault (or *bóveda*) is comprised of bricks overlapping steel beams in a series of semi circular arches, one positioned directly behind the other to resemble a tunnel. Time consuming and very expensive to create, the use of the *bóveda* in various indoor and outdoor structures dates to ancient Egypt. It was the Roman's complex use of the barrel vault that provided the basis for the varied and intricate Gothic forms of the Middle Ages which reached their zenith in the iconic stone roofs of Romanesque churches. In many states, the expense associated with the *bóveda* has led to its demise, however, the evocative style remains popular in the state of Jalisco where it has become the preserve of a clique of elite craftsman as many masons have, for financial necessity, moved on to more lucrative vocations.

Detail shot of bóveda in dining room

Hallway to master bedroom

A work of brilliance and dexterity, a bóveda ceiling arches majestically above the first floor hallway. As well as providing architectural unity with the living spaces below, the bóveda sets the mood for the exquisite colonial features that define the master bedroom.

En suite bathroom

At Casa Dos Cisnes, the natural and material worlds coalesce with grace and majesty. The ocean forms an integral part of the home's architectural elements. Here, in the ensuite bathroom on level three, a tapestry of violet talavera tiles merges seamlessly with the aqua marine ocean below. Over the sinks, also embellished with talavera tiles, hangs a hand-carved silver leaf mirror.

Talavera Tiles

Islamic culture introduced glazed tiles to Spain even before the Muslim invasion of the 8th century; ceramics performed a structural function in the form of unglazed bricks, roofing tiles and water channels. The use of such tiles soon spread from Spain throughout the Western world. In Spain, as early as the 17th century, the name "*Talavera*," after the Spanish ceramic center of *Talavera* de la Reina, became synonymous with glazed pottery. From stairway risers to bathroom sinks or kitchen and wall friezes, the infinite colors and designs—floral, eclipse, solid, saw tooth, or *medio pañuelo*—of *talavera* tiles are emblematic of the ever-enduring and highly fashionable Mexican design ethos. In addition to radiating warmth and adding beauty, the Mexican *talavera* tile is a highly functional and low maintenance art form prized for its longevity. At Casa Dos Cisnes, lustrous walls of *talavera* tiles transform the ordinary into the extraordinary, adding vivid color, texture and contrast to every conceivable space.

Kitchen

Medio-pañuelo talavera *tiles form a picture window frame that opens on to a lush garden complete with a captivating stone fountain.*

Bathroom with *Talavera* tiles

To create a stunning mosaic of talavera *tiles in a bathroom requires planning and perseverance. In addition to their aesthetic appeal,* talavera *tiles add historicist elements to any home or building and are sufficiently hardy to last for generations.*

Nichos in terraza comedor

A remarkable collection of religious artifacts embellishes the eight nichos of the terraza comedor and brings the space to life.

Nichos

Nichos are a common architectural feature both inside and outside Mexican homes. Traditionally designed to showcase the family's favorite saint, nichos provide the ideal opportunity to transform negative spaces into positive. At Casa Dos Cisnes, nichos house the owner's exquisite collection of religious artifacts that embrace both their faith and their passion for Mexico colonial design.

Montage - Detailed images of *nichos*

Staircase

A dramatic spiral staircase forms one of the villa's most dramatic architectural features. A series of nichos showcase more of the owner's collection of religious icons and artifacts.

Water Features

In a typical Spanish colonial home, rooms were assembled around a central courtyard that was animated with Mudéjar-style water features that reflected the artistic legacy of the Moor's conquest over Christian Spain. In Islamic culture, water plays both a physical and metaphysical role. Necessary for irrigation and drinking, water was also required for ablution (ritual purification) and bathing as part of daily spiritual practice.

The rich symbolism and harmonizing influence of water plays a major role in the interior design and ambience of Casa Dos Cisnes. An enclosed passageway, or *zaguán*, serves as a threshold that divides the street from the villa's central courtyard. A stone fountain nestled among flowers and plants acts as the home's axis point, a unifying frame of reference for each level of the home. On entering the villa, the mellifluous sound of water simultaneously soothes and energizes mind and body. The fountain's counterpart, a stunning weeping wall unites the elemental force of water with the villa's arresting religious iconography. Recalling an Islamic prayer site, the villa's two weeping walls impart a divine aura that invites contemplation and cultivates a break from the material world.

Entrance garden fountain

In the entrance garden, a gently bubbling hand-carved cantera *fountain with a* talavera *tiled basin immediately establishes* Casa Dos Cisnes *as a haven of tranquility.*

Weeping wall

Recalling a holy shrine, there's something restorative and mind altering about the weeping wall, with a floating cantera *carving of the Casa Dos Cisnes house insignia, that provides the backdrop for intimate, romantic dinners and ebullient family gatherings in the main dining room.*

Fountain

A modern day Eden, the fountain provides the enchanting focal point for the courtyard's third level. As well as furnishing the media/game room and three bedrooms with a harmonious soundtrack, the courtyard's lush vegetation and elemental aura blurs the boundaries between inside and outside worlds.

Outdoor fireplace

On the master bedroom terrace, the outdoor fireplace creates a warm and romantic ambience. Stunning in its simplicity, grey cantera *stone surrounds the hearth, which is juxtaposed against a vivacious ocher stucco wall. Above the fireplace, the Casa Dos Cisnes emblem is carved from* cantera *stone and recalls the home's genesis as a magical place suspended in time: "The House of the Two Swans."*

Fireplace

The Spanish colonial-style fireplace provides functional warmth in the cool winter evenings, inspires decorative expression and adds transformative power to the ambience of any living space. When it comes to the style and material of the colonial-style fireplace, Mexican homes vary tremendously from fireplaces elaborately framed with cantera stone or plain stucco, raise brick hearths or talavera-encrusted mantles. Fire screens and implements are traditionally fashioned from wrought iron cast in swirling arabesques or intricate floral patterns that echo the carvings on a cantera stone surround.

Living Room Fireplace

As the focal point of the main living area, the fireplace unites the colonial features of the home and magnetically draws guests together for pre-dinner drinks or after dinner conversation. Above the mantel, a colonial-style painting and flickering candelabras impart a noble ambience.

Chapter 3
Casa Dos Cisnes - A Way of Living

Part 1
Entertaining Spaces

*G*ourmet dining is central to life at Casa Dos Cisnes. Throughout the home, a series of well conceived entertainment spaces, each with their own unique aura, serve as a luxurious backdrop to delectable epicurean dishes conjured by the in-house chef each day: an al fresco smorgasbord of antojitos; a candlelit dinner for two; a family gathering or celebration; fiestas; weddings; baptisms; and fashion shoots.

Warm and inviting, the villa's formal main dining room, located between (and often expanded to include) the courtyard and wrap-around covered terrace is dedicated to sensory indulgence. In this ebullient space, an endless stream of family, friends and guests convene at sunset for cocktails, followed by a Mexican culinary odyssey accompanied by inspired conversation. Anchored by an aged wooden table and a magnificent chandelier, the dining room's design statements reflect the owners' appreciation for understated grandeur. Bracketed by a charming garden with a weeping wall and centerpiece fountain chiseled from *cantera* stone, the dining room's soothing water features pay homage to Mexico's colonial history and find affinity with the lushness of the Pacific Coast's tropical landscape.

Nighttime view of dining area

At night, the living/dining area reveals the transformative effects of lighting. Elegant candelabras cast shadows over talavera *dishes and hand-blown glass goblets. Lush palms swoon before an illuminated* cantera *stone archway that frames the brilliant indigo moonlit sky. Fresh flowers set the delightful mood for an epicurean indulgence of the highest order.*

Every artifact, furnishing or design element has been carefully selected according to its unique function or symbolic value. The ornate wooden frame houses a mirror, strategically positioned to ensure all dinner guests luxuriate in the villa's sublime ocean views. In the living area, a *cantera* stone fireplace transitions the villa from its outward looking daytime disposition, which is defined by the home's proximity to the ocean, to its warm and cozy nocturnal mien: a harmonious world unto itself.

Casa Dos Cisnes' myriad outdoor entertainment spaces include a covered patio (or terraza comedor) on the second (main) floor, the master terrace on the top floor and the pool terrace/bar grill on the lowest level. The owners cleverly designed each outdoor space to allow for impromptu meals and spontaneous gatherings enveloped by the villa's spellbinding natural environment.

Versatility forms one of the essential tenets of Casa Dos Cisnes' design philosophy. Each living and dining space can be adapted to suit small or large parties and promote intimacy or formality on a grand or small scale. And, with yet another stroke of design ingenuity, cozy alcoves, cantera stone archways, a separate sitting area and a retreat room provide refuge, a space to which guests can withdraw for intimate conversation or rest while remaining within the unifying public space.

Sitting Room

A sitting area provides an intimate space separate from (but still integrated with) the social nexus of the main living/dining area. A leather sofa and upholstered armchairs sit comfortably with the colonial-style hand-carved bookcase.

Dining Room Table

The dining room table, custom designed to expand or contract to accommodate the number of guests, provides for a refined yet intimate dining experience.

Terrace

Casa Dos Cisnes' sweeping open terraces, replete with jaw-dropping views, can accommodate wedding parties and other large events.

Dining Room

In the Mexican colonial-style home, the mesa *(table) provides the quintessential gathering place for family meals and instills a sense of nurturing and nourishment that goes far beyond the kitchen. As the focal point of every home, the mesa is venerated as the locus of family life and, therefore, the most essential item of furniture. At Casa Dos Cisnes, the dining table can be expanded to comfortably seat 12 people.*

Part 2
Casa Dos Cisnes: A Culinary Fantasia/La Cocina

When it comes to gourmet cuisine, Mexico produces molecular gastronomy without even trying. A land where all things fresh and local rule, Mexican cuisine, whether at a roadside stand or in a venerable restaurant, delivers the kind of religious experience that transcends those much coveted Michelin constellations. With menus laced with the piquant flavors that define Mexico's complex cultural heritage, it's not hard to appreciate how, in 2010, Mexico's traditional cuisine joined the haute gastronomy of France on UNESCO's representative list of 'Intangible Cultural Heritage of Humanity.'

Out on the streets and in the markets, the Pacific Coast's culinary fantasia is revealed. Mexico's exhilarating landscape, which encompasses pristine beaches, tropical forests, dry deserts, fertile valleys and snowcapped mountains, is home to an incredible diversity of ingredients. For the most part, Mexico has yet to be gripped by industrial agriculture; everything is, by necessity, local and sustainable. Everywhere you go, you'll encounter impossibly fresh, Jurassic-sized ingredients, centuries-old secret recipes and the ancient Aztecs and Maya's flair for sauces.

Over the last decade, Puerto Vallarta, with its delectable fusion of high and low culinary techniques, not to mention its stunning tropical setting, has become a hot culinary destination seducing globetrotting gourmands the world over. There are now eight restaurants that boast the prestigious Five Star Diamond Award in recognition of their superb gastronomy.

For many guests who visit the owners' luxurious hill top retreat, epic dining forms part of a regional food pilgrimage. With Casa

Kitchen

Pine cabinetry, talavera tiles, Saltillo flooring and a classic indigo and white zigzag tile color combination are common features of Mexican colonial-style kitchens. The villa's inside-outside philosophy is expressed once again in a picture widow framed with talavera tiles that opens onto a tranquil garden with a centerpiece cantera stone fountain.

Dos Cisnes' sublime natural setting and romantic entertaining spaces, it's hard to imagine a better place to indulge in inspired nouveau Mexican cuisine courtesy of the villa's in-house chef. From *huevos rancheros* to chicken draped in fragrant *mole*—that material expression of the Mexican spirit—or sublime seafood, ranging from red snapper *zarandeado* to tuna steak or giant shrimp seared on the grill, every meal offers a fascinating fusion of native culinary traditions and modern gastronomic techniques.

At Casa Dos Cisnes, the well-proportioned kitchen is a functional space that operates as the chef's personal laboratory rather than a social hub/gathering space. With its harmonious marriage between modern amenities and traditional colonial features, *la cocina* encapsulates the philosophy of Casa Dos Cisnes: a triumvirate of comfort, style and tradition. At Casa Dos Cisnes, every architectural element and design detail works together to ensure sensual gratification and root the home within the history, context and landscape of Mexico. Top-of-the-line stainless steel appliances are juxtaposed with curvaceous clay pots and boldly colored *talavera* tiles that recall the riotous colors and exoticism of the market place. Behind the kitchen island, a picture window opens to reveal the home's lush garden as nature's invigorating scents mingle with the piquant aroma of *chile* emanating from pots bubbling on the *brasero* stove uniquely set into a polished concrete counter top.

Terraza comedor/Dining terrace

With innumerable outdoor patio spaces, every ritual at Casa Dos Cisnes attains divine status. Served on the covered patio, a leisurely breakfast begins with locally roasted coffee beans, a bounty of fruit and freshly squeezed juice, pastries and freshly baked bread, Made-to-order egg specialties, pancakes or French toast complete the indulgence.

Taste of Mexico

At Casa Dos Cisnes, sauces, marinades and dressings spiked with habanero, epazote, achiote *paste,* ancho chili *and* hierba santa, *remain faithful to Mexico's culinary heritage.*

Caprese Salad

The menu at Casa Dos Cisnes focuses on light, flavorful dishes that incorporate only the finest and freshest seasonal produce.

Table settings

The formal dining area takes a folkloric turn with its talavera ceramic place settings and hand-woven place mats.

Mahi Mahi

A menu highlight: locally caught fish of the day. Here, seared Mahi Mahi fish is marinated in sesame oil and dill and draped with sautéed mushrooms.

Pollo relleno estilo Casa Dos Cisnes

Chicken with a light filling of goat cheese and spinach, surrounded by a poblano cream sauce with accents of chipotle.

Part 3
Thoroughly Modern Villa

Casa Dos Cisnes marries timeless classicism and high-tech modernism with flair. With a focus on sensual pleasure, the villa's principal living areas and outdoor spaces, including an infinity pool, gym, garden and pool bar/patio, liberate mind and body from material concerns. From feather beds draped with high count Egyptian cotton sheets, to the master suite's Jacuzzi tub, and luxurious bathrooms with captivating views, every detail of the home is designed to allow guests to experience one indulgence after another. While relaxation and getting off the grid are synonymous, there's no denying that technology drives the modern world and promotes that sense of wellbeing derived from feeling connected to family and culture. Summoning what could be interpreted as a Mexican iteration of Feng Shui, Casa Dos Cisnes' architectural arrangements create an environment that blends the two states of being–material and spiritual–into one harmonious entity.

One floor below the home's principal living areas, a media room limits accessories to key pieces that give the space an airy expansive feel. Framed by a cabinet made from rustic wood boards salvaged from an abandoned hacienda, a 65-inch flat screen TV, equipped with a

Pool area/ sitting area/ terrace

The pool terrace offers the very finest in outdoor living. Appointed with contemporary wicker furniture, a fully equipped bar area and a large grill, it offers the perfect setting for families and couples to enjoy each other's company and reconnect. The villa's contemporary amenities coalesce with cantera *stone, which frames magnificent ocean views. Cushions in vibrant orange hues reflect the patio's ocher paintwork and blazing sunsets.*

Bose sound system, provides the room's focal point. From Monday night football to the Stanley Cup finals, election night, Wimbledon tennis or a movie night for the children, the media room's state-of-the-art technology allows for an immersive home theater experience. Traditional board games and puzzles provide the opportunity for interactive family entertainment. Throughout the media room, the layering of rustic textures creates a soothing visual rhythm that is comfortable enough for a three-hour film or for children to play and yet sophisticated enough for formal entertaining.

The Bose lifestyle system in the media room provides both media room entertainment as well as music to the main dining/living room, gym and pool levels so families and loved ones can rock or chill out while working out, lounging, or dining.

On the top floor, adjacent to the master bedroom and bath, the retreat room also features a Bose lifestyle system which allows superior quality sound to set the mood for relaxation and romance throughout the master suite.

On the lowest level of the home, surrounded by lush tropical forests, the villa's Edenic garden feels a world away from the lively street life of Puerto Vallarta that unfurls in the distance.

Pool

With views over jungle, coast and gardens, the mesmerising infinity pool is solar heated and blends seamlessly with the azure Pacific Ocean below. On the patio, a riot of bougainvillea flowers pour from barro pots.

Media Room

The media room is a showcase for the villa's state-of-the-art technology, which sits happily with whimsical folkloric handicrafts. A symmetrical arrangement of furniture mirrors the balance and serenity of the adjacent courtyard. A custom L-shaped concrete built-in bench is dressed with white linen cushions while vivacious hand-woven pillows add playfulness.

Gym

It's hard to atone for the day's indulgences when even the villa's air conditioned gym boasts sublime views over Bandera Bay. With free weights, commercial grade exercise machines and yoga paraphernalia, mind and body find space and time to recalibrate.

Pool bar

Take an evening swim in the pool then enjoy a tequila-laced cocktail in the poolside bar before an epic dinner prepared by the in-house chef.

Terrace view

With its sparkling bays and indigo waters fringed with jungle-clothed mountains, Casa dos Cisnes' harmonious design harnesses the Pacific Coast's iconic scenery at every turn.

The epicenter for afternoon recreation and relaxation, the infinity pool is one of the site's favorite respites from the day's heat. Resembling a sheet of glass, the solar-heated pool hovers miraculously over the terraced ledge of the cliff face and invites a refreshing dip (cocktail in hand) regardless of the hour. The covered bar and grill area across from the pool offers an alternative from the piercing sun as well as the opportunity to imbibe in a refreshing drink while catching the latest news or sports event on the 60 inch television.

High speed internet access on each floor of the home ensures connectivity for web surfing and emailing to one's heart's desire. And should someone need assistance or dearly miss friends and family back home, the villa's phones allow guests to easily contact staff as well as call the U.S., Mexico, and Canada throughout the house.

Casa Dos Cisnes' ability to blend modern technological amenities seamlessly with traditional Colonial elegance creates the perfect backdrop for modern living, allowing effortless relaxation to coexist with today's desire for continuous connectivity.

Conclusion

Casa Dos Cisnes is more than just a luxurious home; it is a state a mind. From the moment guests walk through the door and enter the traditional interior courtyard, the 'House of Two Swans' elicits an immediate sense of place, of tradition, and of timeless ritual. The home invites an encounter and a life-long connection with authentic Mexico.

Casa Dos Cisnes embodies the concept that living surrounded by beautiful art, artifacts, and nature enriches your life. Inspired by its environment in its architecture and interior design, each living space is designed in harmony with the outside world. From walls awash with warm salmon and russet hues reflecting the sunset to blue mosaic tiles that blend seamlessly with the ocean, the home was created as a dialogue with its wild and stirring setting. An organic whole, the interior elements, from the natural stone flooring to the cantera columns and sweeping vista terraces, are engineered to maximize the stunning views of the pristine coastline, with a flamboyance of biodiversity directly below.

Steeped in timeless indigenous traditions and rituals, Casa Dos Cisnes' homage to Mexico finds expression in the owners' artfully sourced bespoke pieces, antiques, paintings, and collector's items. But, for all its polish, precision, and impeccable style, the home manages to evoke an elegant and comfortable family environment, enveloping guests with a harmonious aura that invites interaction and relaxation on every level. The balance of ease and aesthetic plays out beautifully with the villa's plush modern amenities, the state-of-the-art technology, and exceptional staff that ensure that every visit to Casa Dos Cisnes will fulfill one's individual needs, desires, or whims.

www.ingramcontent.com/pod-product-compliance
Lightning Source LLC
Chambersburg PA
CBHW040735150426
42811CB00063B/1639